MARGOT

MARGOT

Isabella Margot

MARGOT
Copyright © 2022 by Isabella Margot
All rights reserved. No part of this book may be reproduced, scanned, or distributed in any printed or electronic form without permission.
FIRST EDITION
Interior design by Isabella Margot.
Cover design by Isabella Margot.
Cover photographs by Kira Schwarz, released on pexels.com.
Printed in the United States of America
ISBN: 9798835674398

for the broken ones

DREAMS

dreams

what would you do if i told you
your dreams are reaching for you, too?

DREAMS

stardust

i would cover you in stardust
if you weren't already a star.

DREAMS

cathedral

her body was a cathedral
all lines and curves and apogees
every inch designed to bring you to your knees.

DREAMS

know her

the only way to truly know her
is to know the books she loves and *why*.

DREAMS

birmingham

between their lips stars are born.

DREAMS

one of those girls

she is one of those girls
who makes you feel larger than life:
like anything is possible—
like her wings are strong enough
to hold up her dreams and yours, too.

DREAMS

frost

you will bloom,
and bloom, and bloom,
and bloom again.
origami lotus flower
b l o s s o m i n g
in an ordinary world.

DREAMS

reverie

when i die,
bury me among the ashes
of all the books
that were ever burned.
it will be for me a sea, a reverie,
one last sleep until we meet again.

DREAMS

shipwreck

i have watched you
as you have watched the waves
beat incessantly
against the hull of your ship.
i have watched as you take on water,
patch holes,
curse the sky,
and question the god who made her.
i have seen your struggles
and i have seen your victories.
i have wept with you,
and for you,
and because of you,
and still not a day goes by
when i would not let you wreck yourself
upon my shores.

ISABELLA MARGOT

DREAMS

they call me brielle

i.

i was born with sea water in my mouth.
my first scream sounded of seashells
being crunched like broken glass.
my hair, in the warm summer sun, smells of salt
and shines like pirate's gold.

you think i am weak
because my insides are liquid.

allow me to show you the force water can bring.

allow me to show you how i can boil,

can freeze,

can bring rocks
and rulers and diamonds

to their knees.

DREAMS

they call me brielle

ii.

they call me brielle,
coventina, devi, and damia,
sunset adanova,
andina,
goddess of the wave
and of the water harvest.

without me, the earth would rot
and die.
burn,
and turn to dust
on the dry winds of the east.

so look into my eyes
and tell me if you think you see salvation
or destruction.

for you may be the death of me,
but i will surely be the death of you.

ISABELLA MARGOT

DREAMS

forgetting

learn to leave a room
and then not think about it
(or anyone that was in it)
(or anything that was said in it).
focus on where you are now.

sometimes forgetting is a strength,
not a weakness.

DREAMS

sadness

i can feel my lashes against my cheek
like violin strings playing a sad song
just for me.

DREAMS

venice

venice doesn't speak to everyone. for most, she lies silent, as if trapped between the surface of the water and the bridges that bind her. she knows which tourists cannot smell her perfume over the hot stench of summer fish and sweat so she lets them shuffle their feet down her narrow, winding streets to nothing more than the sound of their own 'ooo's and 'aaaah's. it is for the dreamers she waits. she saves her truths for these lovers of mystery who are unafraid to live in the tension between left and right, up and down, life and death. it is for these wild, wandering souls she unfurls her scent like diamonds on diaphanous sails. she chases them around dark corners and up steep steps, whispering, tantalizing, beckoning with desire. she opens for them like a chest full of treasure. she arches her back beneath them like a promise, a prayer, an invitation to understand each bridge that stretches and breaks across her body—through her, beneath her, above her—is ever pushing, ever pulling, ever drawing together parts of the same whole. this is the venice dreamers know. this is the mystery they feel in their bones. they understand she is a paradox of impossible proportions: she is half land, half sky, half sea and can never be any less of one than she is all three. so, fellow wanderer, if you ever find yourself chosen, may i encourage you to drink and drink deeply. drink!, be merry!—*and look for me.*

ISABELLA MARGOT

DREAMS

moon goddess

if there is a goddess of the moon,

tell her i, too, know what it is like
to take someone else's light
and make it my own.

        tell her i, too,
                p u s h

and   p u l l
    against

        g r a v i t y

    as i spin
    and twist
                   and rotate

around a place

that will never be my home.

ISABELLA MARGOT

DREAMS

goddess of the hunt

i find my crazy in the night,
let the wind howl
across the cool sands of the nearest shore i find,
rip my clothes,
rend my mind.

you think you know me.

in another world, in another life,
you might hold my naked body to the light,

but this world is my domain
this crown is mine to bear:
only i can ride the golden lion.
only i can shoot the golden flare.

they thought the cycle was broken
they thought the devil had won
but a phoenix rises from the ashes

she and i are one.

ISABELLA MARGOT

DREAMS

spring

at
last
it
is

spring

and i am new again.

Part

TWO

REVENGE

REVENGE

social media

crossing off fake friends
like you-know-who's boyfriends
here today, gone tomorrow
it's as easy as one click: unfollow
or maybe i'll just block you
give you a taste of losing true-blue
oh, you think ur smart with the internet?
sneaking around, tryna see my shit?
sorry bitch,
i went private.

REVENGE

suburban saints

you want religious freedom
without religious tolerance.

you strive to be saints
but don't leave your churches.

you know no sinners
beyond those that look like you.

you want a holy life without the strife
of loving an "unholy people."

you are the talk-talkers
shunning the walk-walkers,
the others,
the not-good-enoughs.
and the in-betweens.

you are suburban saints
debating salvation
amongst yourselves
locked up safe and tight
in your house upon a hill.

ISABELLA MARGOT

REVENGE

christmas eve

i.
where is your god tonight?
is he lying in a manger?
or is he with his hands
o u t s p r e a d
over your quietly bowed head
as you take communion
surrounded by family
and friends?

ii.
i'm shaking tonight
on christmas eve
as i hit my knees
because i'm praying your god is in texas
washing the feet of child refugees
not hanging out beneath
your perfectly trimmed tree
or in your (repetitive) resolutions:
omg!!!
#newyearnewme

ISABELLA MARGOT

REVENGE

session whore

let's get one thing straight
my husband's heart is made of gold.
mine is as black as sin.
he'll nod, forgive you
while i daydream about smacking you,
spreading your scandals on the internet,
making sure others won't call you,
or work with you,
or think you're cute.
relax, he's a good man. he won't let me.
cause i'm a bulldog
i'll yell and scream all day
if you piss me off.
but listen,
i see you
i see the real you
and it's worse than if you were plastic
you're a tactic
and i'm gonna attack it:
you think where you're at is pure luck?
when you're treating all the boys
like they're gonna get their dicks sucked?
how you gonna call everybody
your best friend?
that's crazy!

ISABELLA MARGOT

REVENGE

you're manic.
you can't even finish your own sentences
you're spastic
trying to rope me into talking shit about ▮▮▮▮
you're crazy!
you think i'd give you any leverage
to go behind my back
and manipulate me?
bitch, you are fake.
you're ungrateful.
you'd better be glad i'm not famous—
didn't record you
sitting on my couch
talking shit about nashville royalty.
you think you're sooo talented.
girl, you stand on the backs of giants!
you're lucky you even know the ▮▮▮▮
and you better believe if i had a tape recording
i'd kim k your ass
so fast
it'd make your head spin
round and round and round again.
so get your laughs in
cause next time around
you're gonna get your face bashed in
bitch, you know you askin'
but i'm gonna lie in wait

ISABELLA MARGOT

REVENGE

i'm fastin'.
just wait til i see you again
cause i'm plastic.

gonna smile in your face
and be so nice
it makes you sick.

you know every word of this is about you.

but i'm a bitch, too.
and bitch—
that's how i know you.

ISABELLA MARGOT

REVENGE

#*thisisamerica*

a moment of silence, please,
for america,
the red, white, and blue.

how did your family get here?
mine immigrated, too.

ISABELLA MARGOT

Part THREE

INSPO

INSPO

breast cancer

what will you change
before the world changes it for you?

INSPO

dark side

my darling,
do not forget
to touch
the dark side of the moon
that you are

every so often

touch
what is weird
and wild
and wonderful
about you

so as not to forget
that you are whole.

ISABELLA MARGOT

tortoise & hare

don't be afraid
of what's inside of you
just because *the world* doesn't know
what to do with it.

keep doing
what you know to be true.

let *them* be the ones who must catch up to *you*.

INSPO

phoenix

there is a phoenix inside of you.
unleash her.
burn yourself down to the ground
and rebuild
as many times as it takes
to get it right.

INSPO

nashville strong

she didn't know
how strong she was
until she realized
how far she had come
and how far
she still intended to go.

ISABELLA MARGOT

INSPO

go & grow

you don't have to be afraid
of that which lives
and blooms
and dies
inside of you.
you, my darling,
are a garden;
you must be strong enough
to let things go
and sometimes,
you must be strong enough
to let things grow.

ISABELLA MARGOT

INSPO

glass ceilings

maybe this goes without saying, but
let's shatter the glass ceiling
and the one above it.
let's even shatter
the ceiling above that one
and in the process,
let us not forget
to shatter the ceilings
inside of our selves.

ISABELLA MARGOT

INSPO

prophecy

she was told she'd climb mountains.
no one bothered to mention
how long it would take
or how many times
she'd want to quit
along the way.

ap

you may be "in-your-own-way" today,
but over these nascent years
i have seen you grapple
and grow
like kudzu
across the discarded corpses of
your former selves
with a ferocity and a voracity
that is only matched
by your gentle spirit
and your kind heart.
oh, my darling,
though i be not near,
climb still.
climb with—
or without—fear.
for this, like every,
is your spring.
this is your year.

ISABELLA MARGOT

INSPO

still

she was a hard woman,
but she was still a woman.
she'd had a hard life,
but she was still alive.

INSPO

rebirth

what is this thing?
this thing called living?
is it not dying?
are they not both one and the same?

"how will you live?" they ask me.
"the same way i die," i reply,

"for i have died not once, but a thousand times."

INSPO

girl talk

there are things you should know about:

if you stop chasing them,
they will notice you.
you will want them
because they can't love you.
they will pay attention
if you talk dirty and
give good blowjobs.

but what i want you to know is this:

the one for you is not afraid
of your muchness
or your brokenness.

he will go in search of you
even if you are right in front of him.

he will not manipulate you,
control you,
or belittle your body.

you should know there are many truths.
life is about deciding which one will be yours.

ISABELLA MARGOT

INSPO

what if

what if you only sought things that
garnered your own approval?

INSPO

identity

what would you say
if you knew no one would walk away
what would you do
if you knew no one would laugh at you
who would you be
if you knew you could always feel free?

Part

FOUR

PARIS

PARIS

ring the alarm

there is nothing
more alarming
than being in paris
and feeling nothing.

PARIS

notre dame

i must see her in night or in day.
beneath her facade
i am a stowaway.
i cling to her,
i close my eyes and pray.
she is my beacon,
my siren,
my cabernet & hemingway.

ISABELLA MARGOT

PARIS

the latin quarter

on my second trip to paris, i was sitting at a café in the latin quarter with four classmates sipping espresso under a cloud of innocence and cigarette smoke. i was eighteen at the time and that smell—the smell of coffee and marlboros and friendships that i knew would never last—became a marker for me in my life. it has followed me as i have followed it; and so we have circled each other as only dreams and lovers can do.

PARIS

shakespeare & co

she ages
like the books
she loves:
faded—
and worn
at the edges.

inscription inside **the catcher in the rye**

lil j,

the hardest journey we'll ever make
is the one inside ourselves.

the hardest task we'll ever face
is to share the truth of our selves
with others.

remember always,

called or not called: god will be there.

xo

PARIS

lady in waiting

the sun is rising over paris,
city of white,
arms open wide.
through fire and fever
she awaits her lovers:
the ever-patient,
all-knowing bride.

bathed

sometimes
i feel like
my whole life
is about
getting back
to how i feel
when i am in paris.

paris looks good on everyone.
there is no one
who is more beautiful
than when they are bathed
in the city of light.

PARIS

les fleures

on our first day in paris together, he bought me flowers in a store full of books because he thought they would tell me great stories. i put them in a glass full of water and listened closely to their tales of people who were sad, people who were happy, and people who just wanted to make amends. late that night, when the city lights were bright i asked them if they were scared to die; if they were mad that they'd been cut for the pleasures of men. they said they were born to bloom and what better way to live and die than to bring comfort to someone's eyes. i told them they were lovely and i wished them they never had to go. they said *we know, we know.* the day they died, i sat in a café, hid behind my american sunglasses, and cried.

eve

she was poison, prayer, and elixir.
at night she'd mumble—
dare me to fix her.
by day she'd say,
"don't stay.
it's better that way."
so nightly i'd do
the only thing i knew:
i'd drink deep,
hit my knees,
and kiss her.

ISABELLA MARGOT

PARIS

bordeaux

she murmured something
about the red in the bordeaux
staining her lips…
or her life…
i cannot remember which.
i was in love with one—entranced by the other—
and cared not what color they were:
only that they might one day too
stain my lips,
my life.

ISABELLA MARGOT

Part

FIVE

~~LOVERS~~
GHOSTS

~~LOVERS~~
GHOSTS

secrets

i find you here
crawling up the sides of the page
twisting yourself between my letters
like smoke in a glass cage.
i b r e a k.
my heart has secrets not even i can take.

~~LOVERS~~
GHOSTS

fairytales

every fairy tale has a monster or two.
in this story,
one was me.
one was you.

~~LOVERS~~
GHOSTS

reckless

reckless woman,
warrior child,
guard your heart
if you must play with fire.

~~LOVERS~~
GHOSTS

Ma chérie am'Our

i'm so glad you're gone now;
and i'm so thankful
for every inch of the art
i am squeezing
from the g a p i n g throat
of your discarded ghost.

ISABELLA MARGOT

~~LOVERS~~
GHOSTS

battle lines

battle lines drawn around coffee shops,
tennessee,
npr,
you and me.

~~LOVERS~~
GHOSTS

atticus

i guess
i will love you
glittering
in that forgotten doorway
in my own way
forever.

~~LOVERS~~
GHOSTS

summer skin

clinging to my summer skin
like the lies you told that i live so desperately in.

i want to believe in beautiful things.

~~LOVERS~~
GHOSTS

certain choices

i am no different than any one else.
i hear a certain song
and it reminds me of a certain person.

oh, but that person is you
and i know my memories of you
like i know the feel of my pillowcase
against my cheek,
like i know the taste of a ripe strawberry
against my tongue.
and if the moonlight is right,
i can almost see you
in between the sheets
next to me.

either i am mad or i am haunted
and i know not which i prefer to be
if my only choice is
you not here with me.

ISABELLA MARGOT

~~LOVERS~~
GHOSTS

masked rider

your name rides silently:
a masked giant
atop the clouds of judgment
cutting through the joys of my life.

should it not also come with the stopping of clocks,
the weeping and gnashing
of teeth?

~~LOVERS~~
GHOSTS

woodbine

craving thai
missing you

ISABELLA MARGOT

~~LOVERS~~
GHOSTS

on skeletons

i don't know how to write them—
to sort them out for you.
the truth is,
after so much time,
they all look the same
and
i'm afraid—
because it feels safer this way.

ISABELLA MARGOT

~~LOVERS~~
GHOSTS

untitled

she has that look in her eye:
the one that says she's been hurt before
and still doesn't know why.

~~LOVERS~~
GHOSTS

ghosts

of all the ghosts left dancing in my head
you're the only one
i wish weren't dead.
why does glass have to shatter so violently?
how can you exist in my head
so loudly
and yet
so silently?

ISABELLA MARGOT

~~LOVERS~~
GHOSTS

sizes

for a long time
i thought you cruel,
hardhearted—
intentionally so.
and then one day i realized:
for me,
you could have swallowed the sun,
the stars,
every bit of galaxy dust,
and everything that made what is ours ours,
but you leaving me
had nothing to do
with how big you were in my world
and everything to do
with how small i was in yours.

~~LOVERS~~
GHOSTS

exit me

exit me
when the sky is grey
and the window dreary
i have grown weary of this war.

~~LOVERS~~
GHOSTS

addiction

i'm addicted to my sadness.
melancholy
fills up
all the empty spaces
in my brain.
even the sunshine can't chase it away.

~~LOVERS~~
GHOSTS

seal, shakespeare, sangre

    even when a rose is dead
    you can still feel its thorns.

~~LOVERS~~
GHOSTS

matches

i will light what can be lit
and i will watch it burn without regret.
i kiss everything goodbye.

~~LOVERS~~
GHOSTS

gatsby

i was 33 when i finally understood
why i never loved the great gatsby.
you see, i'm daisy
but gatsby never comes for me.

~~LOVERS~~
GHOSTS

jordan baker

it may be raining
and it may be may
but there is no jordan baker
and no house across the bay.

~~LOVERS~~
GHOSTS

forgotten

i stared at your face forever
and i couldn't remember your name.
i don't know if that means i forgave you
or if i just forgot you.

ISABELLA MARGOT

~~LOVERS~~
GHOSTS

une oda à la fin d'une amour

i guess i survived you.
but i guess you survived me, too.

supongo que yo te sobreviví.
pero supongo que tú también me sobreviviste.

~~LOVERS~~
GHOSTS

her eyes

her life says happy but her eyes say sad
soul weighed down
with all the successes
she hasn't had.

~~LOVERS~~
GHOSTS

death of a loved one

you killed
all the pieces
i loved about me.

~~LOVERS~~
GHOSTS

ptsd

i gave myself ptsd
trying to make you love me.

~~LOVERS~~
GHOSTS

surgery

one day i will cut you out of me
and the knife will leave no scar.

Part SIX

TWIN FLAMES

TWIN FLAMES

skinny boy

tear me to pieces, skinny boy.

TWIN FLAMES

baby blooms

her breaths come out like flowers. tiny rosebuds!
baby blooms to make me fall in love.

TWIN FLAMES

night-sky body

i reach out
and i touch you with my night-sky body
you open
and let me in

TWIN FLAMES

gardener

you seem to think i am bad at tending roses
(and maybe i am, just a little bit)
but what you don't seem to understand
is how hard it is to keep something alive
that is not meant to survive.

i can supplement the seasons
and all the reasons
a flower should thrive,
but in the end
it will die.

so, no, i do not think the question here
is about my inability to cultivate the impossible
but instead perhaps
about your inability to comprehend reality;

but i do so tenderly love
to see your face externalize your grief
when you realize
all the petals have fallen.

and i can't help but imagine i am the rose
and you the half-adept gardener

ISABELLA MARGOT

TWIN FLAMES

and one day i, too, will wither, then die,
and leave you holding stems that will still prick you
and leaves that will still be green for weeks.

for you, my darling,
have always been the beauty,
while i have always been the beast.

poe

if i told you
i would climb below the earth
to lay with your dead
and rotting body
would you call me crazy?
or think of me
like you think of poe:
dangerous, dark,
and mysterious, but
undoubtedly a genius?

TWIN FLAMES

kisses

late at night,
we drink wine out of thimbles
and make tiny toasts to all the dreams
the world has stolen from us. turns out,
we didn't need them anyway.

ISABELLA MARGOT

TWIN FLAMES

hide & seek

your love snuck up on me.

TWIN FLAMES

private vs. secret

teeth
and tongue
and lips
and mouth
sharp
and wet
and tender.
i'm aroused.

TWIN FLAMES

desire

it was like being seen by the sun.

the radiance of his interest caught me
somewhere between exhale and inhale.

for a second
time
s l o w e d.

and inside that second,
the space between our eyes
contracted,
expanded,
exploded,
fell in on itself,
and caught fire.

a million lifetimes lived inside
one moment of desire.

ISABELLA MARGOT

TWIN FLAMES

star-crossed

and so i choose
to leave what is left for us to another life.
your choices in this one have left me
no other option save death.

marriage

don't be afraid
to fall in love with him again
and again
and again.

don't be afraid
to see him
with new eyes
and a new heart
every new day.

for you, my darling,
are new every morning

doesn't he deserve that, too?

loving you

when i awoke in this world,
i did not know
there was a star
such as your self
waiting for me.
i did not know
there was a kindness
such as yours,
a creature of flesh and bone
who is as delicate
as they are strong.

my love,
my darling,
you prove to me every day
you are more
bright and bold
and brilliant
than i first imagined you to be.
even on my best of days
i could not have guessed that
all the ways i feel
would also be felt by you.

ISABELLA MARGOT

TWIN FLAMES

your love has emboldened me
and made me wise.
i have learned you are the rose,
the storm,
the cliff, and
the precipice of my heart.
and so
i will strip off before you my armor
this armor i have clung to so dearly
through the briars and the oceans
i survived
to make it to you.

to you alone
will i show the scars and stains
that lie beneath this battered breastplate,
this war-weary helmet.

you alone,
my love,
will know
what only i know.
you alone,
my love,
will feel
what only i feel.

ISABELLA MARGOT

TWIN FLAMES

and from this day forward, my love,
your hand and your heart alone,
will be for me a better shield
than any i have ever had before.

loving you
will be the death
of many things,
and the birth
of so many,
many more.

ISABELLA MARGOT

TWIN FLAMES

t'aimer
excerpt from '*loving you*'

t'aimer
serait la mort
de beaucoup de choses,
et la naissance
de beaucoup,
beaucoup plus.

TWIN FLAMES

february

i am girded by gravity
guarded by guides
i wield no weapons
i am *u n d o n e* by your side.
as the fan ruffles your hair
and your breath ruffles my soul,
nighttime draws near.

ISABELLA MARGOT

Part

SEVEN

KNOW THYSELF

KNOW THYSELF

world war me

you see a plate.
i see a battleground crawling with self-hate.

KNOW THYSELF

mood: survivor

i may never outrun my past but i will outlast it.

KNOW THYSELF

motto

do the things that scare you;
but don't be motivated by fear.

KNOW THYSELF

self-love

you are one romance away from it all coming true.
a romance, my dear, with you.

KNOW THYSELF

piles

let the past lie where it fell.
buried or burned,
it did not last.

KNOW THYSELF

serpentine

like a serpent,
i shed my skin.
always urging
new layers to grow in.
as i change,
it expands to cover me.
a quilt of stars:
orion's belt,
ursa major,
earth's moon,
the sun.
can you see them?
look, here on my arm!
look, here, beneath my chin.
can you read it?
this,
the map of my mother's skin
the universe
has wrapped me in.

ISABELLA MARGOT

KNOW THYSELF

new beginnings

a tremble
is the perfect way to start
many things.

KNOW THYSELF

flight

for all the beauty of a bird in flight,
there is a time when your wings can glide the air
and a time when they must fight.

KNOW THYSELF

wrigley james

as i sat and watched you,
i felt my love for you stir—
in my chest,
my
sternum,
my stomach—
and i knew in that instant
some previously hard
and frozen layer
of my cold and ruthless heart
had thawed,
vaporized,
and disappeared.

KNOW THYSELF

what lies betwixt

never question the head-heart connection.
whether physical or physiological—
either way—
your vocal cords lie between them.

KNOW THYSELF

recovery

she finally threw her hands in the air
and yelled for it to stop.

"enough!" she screamed
as she dropped to her knees
to gather the pieces
of herself she had lost.

i asked her, "what changed?"
as we sifted and swayed,
searching through dirt and dust.

with tears in her eyes she softly replied,
"i heard a song i forgot…
one that usually reminds me who i want to be
but this time
it made me see
all of the me
i am not."

ISABELLA MARGOT

KNOW THYSELF

deconstruction

i hate that you took my rebellion
and told me it was a sin.
i hate that you sold me on gentle women
who carry no fire within.
i hate that you told me my tongue
would get me in trouble one day.
i hate that you said i was a pagan
and showed me the 'proper' way to pray.

that's why i've been curled in a corner.
that's why i've been huddled in the dark.
you did more than almost steal my future
you almost stole my spark.

but god sent a rustle of tree limbs
with a wind that stirred my hair
she showed me a vast and dangerous world
that she created with the utmost care.

she took me to the tops of volcanoes
and to the depths of the dangerous seas:
and when she laid me back in bed that night
she said,

ISABELLA MARGOT

KNOW THYSELF

"i made you as wild as these.
　　don't ever think—
　not even for a second—
　i'm anything like them.
i've never been afraid of you
or the fire that burns within."

ISABELLA MARGOT

ACKNOWLEDGMENTS

To those of you who took the time to read MARGOT and to anyone who has ever liked, saved, shared, or reposted my work on social media, thank you.

To my husband, my hurricane, my lighthouse, my anchor: Thank you for loaning me your resilience, your motivation, and your endless belief that we can always be better. No words will ever be enough to capture what you mean to me, but that is not going to stop me from trying.

To my mother, my editor, my biggest fan: I finally did it. Thank you for never giving up on me or any of my projects. Thank you for every sacrifice, for every hug, for every moment together. I am who I am today because of you.

To my Classy Classics Ladies, for me you were the light of Eärendil, and I shall forever be grateful that I had you when I so often felt I had nowhere else to turn.

To Jess, for being so much more than just a girl with a book. You were my bridge into the new, brilliant, and life-giving world of bookstagram. I am in your debt.

To Julia, for the trip to Paris I will never forget, for inspiring "stardust" and "dreams," and for my first ever bulk order.

To Mrs. Tomlin, Ms. Bond, and Ms. Cassidy, for being the kinds of teachers who made me feel seen, heard, inspired, and like I really could survive my hometown.

To AP, one of my favorite photographers and muses.

To Sarah Sedor-George, for the translation of "t'aimer."

To my aunts Rita and Nancy, who, by swiftly and consistently schooling everyone in Scrabble, showed me at a very early age how cool it is to be female, brilliant, and educated.

To my stepbrother Ailin: hey, I did a thing!

To Hilary & Kenny, for being our people.

To Dani, for being a tireless champion of your friends and their art; I do not deserve you, but I am so glad I have you.

To Baylee, for being my person.

To Berly, my HLP. I adore you. Here's to growing old together and still dancing on speakers.

To my dad, for finishing that coin collection, the drink at that bar in Savannah, and for the family trip to Greece. If I have to be in a boat with anyone, I am glad it is with you.

To my brother, for inviting me to write "loving you," for leading me into the world of fantasy literature, and for gifting me "The Collected Poems of Robert Frost." Your fingerprints are scattered across my life in more ways than you will ever know.

And finally, to my alma, mi belleza, my daughter: loving you will be the death of many things and the birth of so many, many more.

Here's to the more, my love.

ABOUT THE AUTHOR

Isabella Margot lives in Lake View, AL with her incredible husband, their wise & wild daughter, and their beloved goldendoodle. Her favorite city is Paris, France and her favorite drink is brut rosé. She is an INFJ and an Enneagram 4w5 (emphasis on the five). Her favorite books are East of Eden, The History of Love, Sister Carrie, and The Starless Sea. Her favorite movies are Ever After, Gattaca, Rigoletto (1993), and Bright Star. She hopes wherever you are, you find the poetry in living.

isabellamargot.com
Instagram & TikTok: @isabellamargot
Facebook.com/isabellamargotpoetry

fin.

Made in the USA
Columbia, SC
27 January 2023